Mama!
Why Do You Have to Go to Work?

Written by Kevin Chin
Illustrated by Hui Ding

DEDICATION

To all the mothers who struggle through the daily heartbreaking moments of leaving their children home so they can make a difference in this world, your courage and sacrifice is incredible.

All rights reserved. No part of this publication maybe reproduced or transmitted or stored in any form or by any means without written permission of the publisher.

Text copyright © 2020 by Kevin Chin
Illustrations © 2020 by Hui Ding
ISBN: 978-1-7357114-0-9

Mama! Why do you have to go to work?

Mama goes to work as a drama teacher to help her students be creative and have the courage to perform on stage!

But, when Mama comes home...

Mama! Why do you have to go to work?

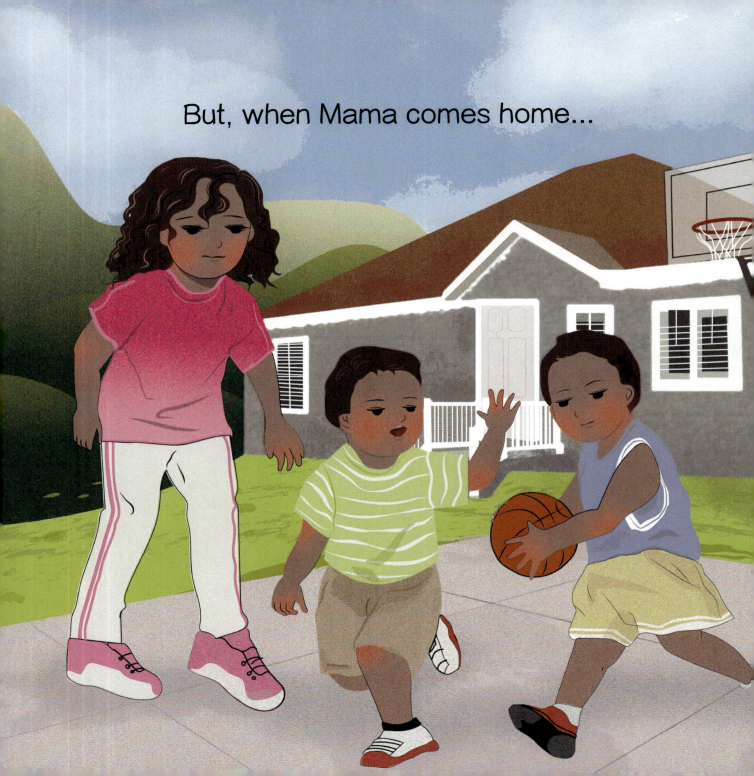

She shows her love by coaching both of you to play fair and have fun!

Mama goes to work as a doctor to help sick people feel better so they can go home to their families as soon as possible!

But, when Mama comes home...

Mama! Why do you have to go to work?

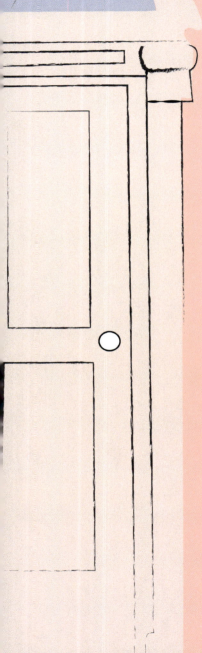

Mama goes to work as a rocket scientist so she can help explore our amazing universe!

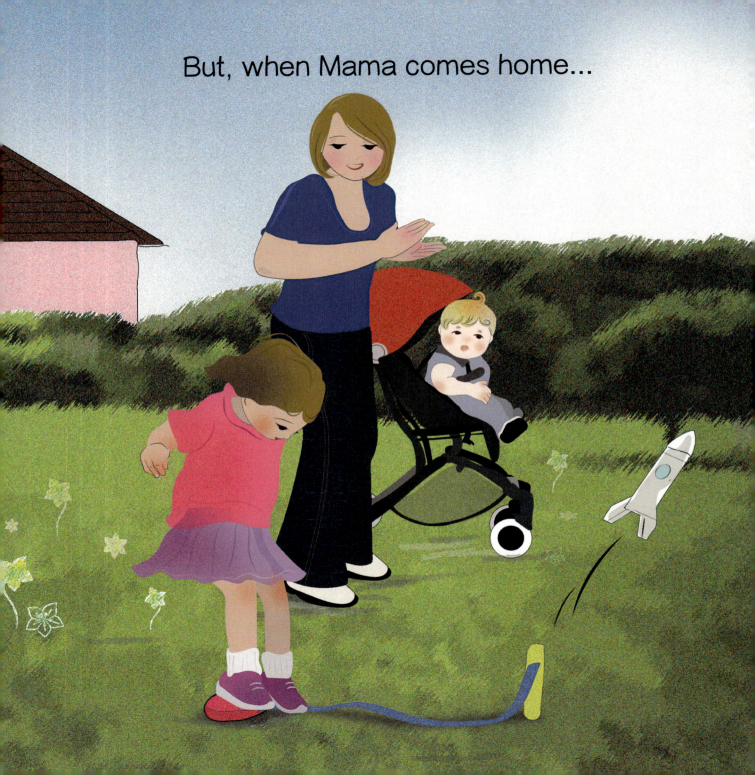

Mama goes to work as a computer programmer to create software that helps people talk and see each other!

But, when Mama comes home...

She shows her love by fixing all of your electronics so you can learn and play.

Just remember, no matter what Mama does when she goes to work⋯ she misses you, just as much as you miss her.

Mama, now I know why you go to work. You go to work so you can share your love by helping people.

Made in the USA
Las Vegas, NV
17 January 2024